Contents

HOW TO FIND INFORMATION

•

ENVIRONMENT

By PAULA S OWEN

How to find information: environment

ISBN 0-7123-0808-3

Published by:
The British Library, Science Reference and Information Service, 1998

© 1998 The British Library Board

Cover photograph: Dave Griffiths

For more information on British Library publications contact Paul Wilson at
the Science Reference and Information Service, 25 Southampton Buildings,
London WC2A 1AW. Tel: 0171-412 7472

DTP by Concerto, Leighton Buzzard, Bedfordshire (01525 378757)

Printed by PMC Printers, PMC House, 118 Stanstead Road, London SE23 1BX.

Chapter 1.   Introduction

This short guide aims to provide the user with enough practical guidance and examples to begin a literature search in the complicated, and often confusing, field of environmental information. The author, Paula S Owen, runs the British Library's Environmental Information Service and has many years of experience disseminating environmental information to a wide variety of information users.

The layout of this guide is as follows: hard copy sources, including most printed source material – books, monographs, journals, grey literature, etc. along with reference sources such as directories, encyclopaedias and yearbooks – are explored in Chapter 3; CD-ROM and online sources are discussed together in Chapter 4; Internet sources, although at a basic level just another form of electronic information, are given their own chapter – Chapter 5 – primarily as a result of the range and depth of environmental information that has become available on the Internet over the past few years.

The final chapter, Chapter 6, is devoted to a description of the role of the Environmental Information Service (EIS). It describes the services offered, together with the environmental publications and seminars available, from the British Library. The Service acts as a gateway to the environmental publications held by the Library and its remit is to help students, teachers, the general public and companies locate environmental data and references quickly and efficiently.

Finally, the limitations of this book must be addressed. As the term 'environment' is so vast in its coverage, it is beyond the remit of a short guide such as this to include in-depth sources for every environmental area, in particular, this guide does not feature environmental standards and legislation. Instead, the most important general sources are mentioned with emphasis being placed on the various mechanisms available for finding information.

For detailed information on individual environmental topic areas, the accompanying publication *Environmental information – a guide to sources* (2nd ed.) is recommended. Details of how to order this publication are included at the back of this guide.

Chapter 2. Problems with Locating Environmental Information

Relevant and timely environmental information may prove troublesome to locate on account of its varied scope, levels of complexity and format. A search can also become very involved if one is looking for an impartial overview of a particular topic rather than one fixed aspect of it. This difficulty results from the varying interpretations applied to environmental data and information by agencies, research groups, charities and pressure groups, who then publish their findings. Some of the difficulties encountered when trying to locate environmental information are outlined below:

Split discipline

Environmental science has only been recognised as a science in its own right for about the last three decades. Previously, it was simply a subset of other, longer established sciences such as chemistry, biology, ecology and geography. The interconnectivity with other sciences makes searching for solutions to environmental issues a multidisciplinary procedure. It can be said that if you were searching for information regarding chemistry or a particular chemical, for example, you would need to consult a chemistry text. However, if you are searching for environmental information you may need to consult not only environmental literature, but also chemistry, engineering, ecology and medical publications.

Subjectivity

As a result of the sometimes emotive, and often controversial, nature of environmental issues, subjectivity becomes more of an issue in this area than any other. Care must be taken to investigate all sides of an environmental problem. For example, an assessment of a planning issue from an environmentalist's point of view would take a very different tone from that of a commercial developer's report on the same problem, even if they both purported to be an 'environmental assessment' of the topic.

Costs and time needed to gather data

Information gathering in this area can be a very costly exercise. For example, field studies and environmental auditing all involve expensive processes and experts to undertake the work. In addition, these studies may take years to complete and analyse. This can be particularly important in measuring the effects of air, soil and water pollution at different localities over various timescales. As a result, the data are sometimes not made available for a number of years after collection. An example of this is the delay in producing the 1992 *Chemical Release Inventory*, published by Her Majesty's Inspectorate of Pollution (HMIP). This document was not available for public scrutiny until September 1994.

Certain restrictions on access

Since 1 January 1993, the UK has implemented regulations regarding freedom of access to environmental information. However, owing to the ambiguities and vague definitions in the original EC *Directive on public access to environmental information* (90/313/EEC), access to certain types of information can still prove difficult. Organisations with special collections may restrict access or charge for their information, although the regulations stipulate that any charge must be a "reasonable" one. Unfortunately, there is increasing pressure on such suppliers of information to recover their costs, especially if their own funding from public money is diminishing. Hence, a "reasonable" charge may include a contribution to the cost of the research, for example, which can prove quite expensive for the individual.

Amount of grey literature

Grey literature abounds in the environmental area and its main drawback is that it is very difficult to trace. Grey literature includes publications that are outside the easily recordable categories such as books, encyclopaedias, dictionaries, periodicals and journals. Examples are conference proceedings, reports, newsletters, bulletins, theses and pamphlets. These publications often contain important information that is not easily found elsewhere, but are not recorded in the standard sources.

Personal contact

Personal contact is often the most useful and timely method of retrieving information. Instead of wasting valuable time searching around for the right book or journal that could take days, one telephone call to the relevant person could answer your query or point you in the direction of the most useful sources of information. The main disadvantage of this source of information is that a good contact list takes time to build up and also people move on and new contacts have to be made. Contacts can be made by keeping abreast of the relevant, current directories in any particular area. Make sure you are looking at the most up-to-date edition and if in doubt ask for, or write to, the position stated in the entry rather than the name attached to it.

To turn to the positive side, the rapid growth of interest in the environment has lead to an equally rapid growth in the supply and availability of environmental information, not only of a scientific and technical nature but also information concerned with legislative, regulatory and commercial activities. This growth in provision is apparent not only in printed and electronic sources but also in the number of organisations offering environmental information services and publications. This can only be an advantage to the environmental enquirer.

Chapter 3.   Printed Sources

There are six general types of printed information sources. These are: books; journals; patents; grey literature; reference works – collectively known as primary sources; and secondary sources, examples of which are abstracting or indexing journals.

Primary sources

Books, monographs and series

These primary sources of information are usually the most extensively advertised and easy to access through bookshops, publishers or libraries.

It would be impossible here to print a comprehensive list of textbooks of environmental interest, and in any case they should not be too difficult to locate. A basic search on any library's catalogue should pick up a number of reference books of interest. A point to keep in mind would be the age of the publication. However, this is not as problematic as with other scientific disciplines because of the relatively short history of environmental research.

If you are investigating a new area, and have no idea of the printed source subject coverage, comprehensive listings of publications can be found in publication directories. These directories are usually classified by geographical area rather than subject coverage. For example, details of US environmental titles can be obtained from the Subject Guide volumes to *Books in Print* (Bowker, 9 vols, 1996-97, ISBN 0-8352-3785-0 or ISSN 0068-0214). There are 40 pages devoted to environmental topics alone, ranging from environmental auditing to environmental tourism. For UK titles, the best source is *Whitaker's Books in Print* (J. Whitaker, 5 volume set, London, ISBN 0-8502-1263-4). The Subject index lists 22 pages, in very small print, of environmental publications produced in the UK. For the rest of the world we have *International Books in Print* (KG Saur, 2 vols, Munich, ISBN 3-598-22133-9) which covers English language titles published in Africa, Asia, Australia, Canada, Continental Europe, Latin America, New Zealand, Oceania and the Republic of Ireland. Unfortunately there is no subject coverage, simply author and title searching.

Both the Bowker and Whitaker publications can also be searched by author and title and may be searched electronically via online and CD-ROM sources. An example of a search through the online *Bowker's Books in Print* database is shown next.

Example I – searching for book titles

An enquirer is interested in receiving a list of books on the topic of *Sustainable tourism*. This is a relatively recent topic of interest within the environmental sector and it is not thought that there will be many books devoted to this subject.

A search strategy was devised, it was decided to look for the key terms: *sustainable development* or *ecotourism* in the title of the books. The database was then consulted. The following output was obtained through the Dialog host system:

```
File 470:Books In Print(r)  1997/Aug
   (c) 1997 R.R.Bowker, Reed Elsevier Inc.
Set  Items  Description
S1   7      (SUSTAINABLE(W)TOURISM)/TI  (/TI restricts keywords to title field)
S2   9      ECOTOURISM/TI
S3   16     S1 OR S2                        (This command combines the 2 sets)
t s3/7/1-16                                 (Displays the retrieved results)

3/7/1
DIALOG(R)File 470:Books In Print(r)
   (c) 1997 R.R.Bowker, Reed Elsevier Inc. All rts. reserv.

   08447873   09163030
   TITLE: Sustainable Tourism: A Global Perspective
   AUTHOR: Harris, Rob; Heath, Ernie; Toepper, Lorin; Williams, Peter
   ISBN: 0-7506-2385-3 (1997/08)
   STATUS: Active Record
   PUBLISHER: Buttrwrth-Heinemann
   PUBLICATION DATE: 121997 (199712)
   NO. OF PAGES: 200p.

3/7/2
DIALOG(R)File 470:Books In Print(r)
   (c) 1997 R.R.Bowker, Reed Elsevier Inc. All rts. reserv.

   08358683   09052034
   TITLE: The Business of Ecotourism: The Complete Guide for Eco-Sensitive
   Tourism Providers
   AUTHOR: Patterson, Carol
   ISBN: 1-879432-25-0 (1997/03)
   STATUS: Active Record
   PUBLISHER: Explorers Guide Pub
   PUBLICATION DATE: 061997 (199706)
   NO. OF PAGES: 200p.
```

TITLE: Sustainable Tourism in Islands & Small States: Issues & Policies
ISBN: 1-85567-370-3 (1995/08)
STATUS: Active Record
VOLUME: Vol. 1
SERIES: Island Studies
PUBLISHER: Bks Intl VA
PUBLICATION DATE: 021996 (199602)
NO. OF PAGES: 256p.

08225703 08885820
TITLE: Sustainable Tourism?: European Experiences
ISBN: 0-85199-100-9 (1996/05)
STATUS: Active Record
SERIES: A C. A. B. International Publication Ser.
PUBLISHER: OUP
PUBLICATION DATE: 101996 (199610)
NO. OF PAGES: 224p.

In summary: books, monographs and series

Advantages

    Easily accessible in libraries and book shops

    Well publicised

    Standard reference in first instance

Disadvantages

    Technology/subject quickly out of date

    New editions take a long time to produce

Other books of interest in this area are dictionaries, encyclopaedias and directories.
A selection of useful examples of the genre can be found later in this chapter.
Again, a search of the publication directories detailed above will identify the most
important publications.

Journals and periodicals

There are thousands of journals that cover environmental subject areas. To help locate the most pertinent and topical periodicals in an area of interest, the most useful information source is *Ulrich's International Periodicals Directory* (Bowker, 5 vols, 1997, ISBN 0-8352-3806-7 or ISSN 0000-0175). This publication allows you to search for titles and ISSNs. It also lists useful information such as title changes, cessations and online/CD-ROM version availability. It does not contain a subject guide.

In addition to the hard copy version, which can be quite cumbersome to search if you do not have specific titles to investigate, there are both online and CD-ROM versions of this publication. These allow greater flexibility in searching techniques. It is possible to search by subject area and general descriptors, allowing for a more comprehensive, and more accurate, search of the topic of interest.

Example 2 – searching for journal titles

A student needs to locate a few important primary journals in the area of environmental wastewater management in the UK. The student has never researched the area before and has no idea of any particular titles to look for.

The student is advised to consult the online version of *Ulrich's International Periodicals Directory* via the Dialog Host, using the *descriptor* and *geographical* field identifiers with an extra check to ascertain whether the journals are *current*.

Example output:

```
Set  Items  Description
S1   15     DC=WASTEWATER OR WASTE(W)WATER    (DC = Descriptor code)
S2   22295 GL=UK                              (GL = Geographical locator)
S3   2      S1 AND S2
S4   2      S3 AND ST=ACTIVE                  (ST = Status of publication)

4/9/1
DIALOG(R)File 480:Ulrich's Int'l Periodicals DIR.
    (c) 1997 Reed Elsevier Inc. All rts. reserv.

0165596 STATUS: Active
    Water and Environment International
        Formerly (until 1991): Water Services: ISSN 0301-7028: (until 1974):
        Water and Water Engineering: ISSN 0043-1168
    Ed. Jim Manson
    PUBLISHER: Argus Business Media Ltd.; Subsidiary of: D M G Exhibitions
        Group Ltd.
```

Queensway House, 2 Queensway, Redhill, Surrey RH1 1QS, England,
   Tel. 44-1737-768611
FIRST PUBLISHED: 1899
FREQUENCY: Bimonthly Circ. 8,600 Microform, from UMI
PRICE: E85 (overseas #87) (effective 1997)
GEOGRAPHIC LOCATION: United Kingdom (UK)
ISSN: 0969-9775 CODEN: WTSVAK
DEWEY DECIMAL CALL NO.: 628 LC CALL NO.: TJ
SPECIAL FEATURES: abstr. illus. stat. tr. lit. index. Book Reviews
ABSTRACTING AND INDEXING SERVICES: Br.Tech. Ind.; Chem. Abstr.;
   Curr. Cont.; Eng. Ind.; Excerp. Med.; Br. Geol. Lit.; Fluidex; GeoRef.; Intl. Civil
   Eng. Abstr.; Soft. Abstr. Eng.; W. R. C. Inf.; IDA; Geo. Abstr. P. G.
Copies provided for fee (C$); No free copying (NC); No free use of
   abstracts to abstracting services (NCA)
LISTED IN: UI – Ulrich's International Periodicals Directory; ST -
   Scientific and Technical Books and Serials in Print
SUBJECT HEADINGS: ENVIRONMENTAL STUDIES-POLLUTION
(00011216);
   ENVIRONMENTAL STUDIES-WASTE MANAGEMENT (0001123X)
Covers water and waste water treatment from an environmental perspective.

4/9/2
DIALOG(R)File 480:Ulrich's Int'l Periodicals DIR.
   (c) 1997 Reed Elsevier Inc. All rts. reserv.

0134694 STATUS: Active
Water Products
Ed. Caroline Ellerby
PUBLISHER: Faversham House Group Ltd.
Faversham House, 232a Addington Rd., South Croydon, Surrey CR2 8LE,
England, Tel. 44-181-651-7100

FIRST PUBLISHED: 1995
FREQUENCY: Bimonthly
PRICE: E31.50 (foreign #57.50 ($92)) (effective 1997)
GEOGRAPHIC LOCATION: United Kingdom (UK)
ISSN: 1359-7361
DEWEY DECIMAL CALL NO.: 628.1 LC CALL NO.: X ; TJ
LISTED IN: UI - Ulrich's International Periodicals Directory; ST -
   Scientific and Technical Books and Serials in Print
SUBJECT HEADINGS: WATER RESOURCES (00002756)

Product information for water and wastewater industry.

One periodical that does warrant special mention is the *ENDS Report* (Environmental Data Services, ISSN 2870-4100). This monthly UK environmental current affairs publication is one of the most popular general environmental news reports available. If a library is to stock one general environmental periodical, this would be the one. It is available as a monthly subscription, but can also be found in most good libraries. It is also now available as an archive CD-ROM, which includes the full text of the ENDS Report from 1992.

Example 3 – a search on the ENDS CD-ROM

A business needs an update on any ENDS articles on the progress of the decommissioning of the Brent Spar oil platform in 1996.

The CD allows the date range to be specified to individual months and years. Hence the enquirer takes advantage of this facility to specify information from January to December 1996. As this search is relatively simple the enquirer simply enters the keywords "Brent Spar" at the search command. Six articles including the keyword "Brent Spar" were retrieved. An excerpt from one of these articles is shown:

256012

ENDS Report: 256   *May 1996*
NERC embarrasses DTI with report on Brent Spar

The Department of Trade and Industry (DTI) has got a good deal more than it bargained for when it commissioned the Natural Environment Research Council (NERC) to advise whether deep sea disposal of the Brent Spar oil installation would be the "best practicable environmental option" (BPEO). NERC's report says that the potential environmental impacts of dumping Brent Spar at sea may not be large enough to exclude this as an option, NERC scientists remain to be convinced that this is the BPEO

The decision to dump the Brent Spar...

In summary: journals and periodicals

Advantages
> Up-to-date reference material
> Front edge of new ideas/discoveries/technology

Disadvantages
> Journal subscriptions have become very expensive
> Availability in libraries is decreasing rapidly
> Time is needed to peruse various journals

Patents

A patent is granted to an inventor to give his/her invention legal protection against exploitation by others in return for full disclosure of the details of the invention. Patents are very important sources of information on technical developments and are often where a new idea first appears in print. Patents cannot be granted if the idea has already been disclosed as the invention to be patented must always be new. Hence a good knowledge of patents is essential to avoid accidental infringement. The best sources of information for patents are the CD-ROM/online databases *INPADOC* and *World Patents Index*.

It has been estimated that 70-80% of the information found in patents is not subsequently recorded in any other form.

In summary: patents

Advantages

Patents are important in technical development as they are often where a new idea first appears in print

c.80% of the information found in patents is not recorded anywhere else

Disadvantages

Difficult to locate if new to patent area

Restricted availability of patents

Complexity of patent document

Grey literature

This term includes literature such as conference proceedings, reports, trade literature, theses and translations. In some environmental areas grey literature is very important and, however difficult it is to track down, no search in such an area can be complete without it. A useful database for such material is the *System for Information on Grey Literature in Europe* (SIGLE) produced by the British Library. The British Library also publishes *British Reports Translations and Theses* (ISSN 0959 4922) which became the *British National Bibliography for Report Literature* in 1998, and the *Index of Conference Proceedings Received* (ISSN 0959 4960) which cover particular aspects of grey literature.

Example 4 – searching for grey literature

Information is required on any grey literature (including governmental publications) on the subject of the Freedom of Environmental Information Act. The enquirer is unsure whether it is a law, directive or set of regulations and is interested in any literature within the EU. The SIGLE database on the British Library Host system BLAISELine is consulted.

The first step is to separate the facets of the search into components. It is decided that *environment or environmental* is one facet; *freedom and information* is a second facet; and *law(s) or regulation(s) or directive(s)* is the third. The truncation/wildcard in this instance is a hash (#). Input is illustrated in bold.

> environment or environmental
TERM (ENVIRONMENT) APPEARS IN (5) CONTEXTS
TERM (ENVIRONMENTAL) APPEARS IN (6) CONTEXTS
SEARCH 1 FOUND 17294 ITEM(S).

> freedom and information
TERM (FREEDOM) APPEARS IN (3) CONTEXTS
TERM (INFORMATION) APPEARS IN (6) CONTEXTS
SEARCH 2 FOUND 34 ITEM(S).

>: 1 and 2
SEARCH 3 FOUND 7 ITEM(S).

>: law# or regulation# or directive#
TERM (LAW#) APPEARS IN (13) CONTEXTS
TERM (REGULATION#) APPEARS IN (6) CONTEXTS
TERM (DIRECTIVE#) APPEARS IN (4) CONTEXTS
SEARCH 4 FOUND 9907 ITEM(S).

> 3 and 4
SEARCH 5 FOUND 6 ITEM(S).

1. RCN - ngb9624139
AP - Roderick$hP – Hallo$hR
EC - Foundation for International Environmental Law and Development (FIELD),
London
EC - In collaboration with Stichting Natuur en Milieu, Utrecht (NL)
TI - Freedom of access to information on the environmental in the United
Kingdom$bA user's guide to the Environmental Information Regulations and*EU
Directive 90/313
PU - $cDec 1994
N28 - Available from British Library Document Supply Centre-DSC:96/29930
N46 - In English

2. RCN - nfr9500816
AP - Haffner$hChristine; Bernard$hChristine; Mormont$hMarc; Sancy$hMary
EC - Ministere de l'Environnement, 92 - Neuilly-sur-Seine (FR). Service de la
Recherche, des Etudes et du Traitement de l'Information sur l'Environnement;
Fondation Universitaire
Luxembourgeoise Belgique (FUL), Arlon (BE)
TI - The European directive on freedom of access to information on environmental
matters : the position of groups in France, Great Britain and Germany in terms of the

transposition of national laws
PU - $c1993
N28 - Available at INIST (FR), Document Supply Service, under shelf-number : RP
185 (3287)

3. RCN - ngb9421688
CI - 1857502124
EC - Friends of the Earth Ltd., London (GB)
TI - Proceedings of a European conference on :Delivering the right to know'$bThe
implications of the Directive on the freedom of access to information on the
environment (90/313/EEC)
PU - $c[1993]
N00 - Conference held London (Great Britain), 2 Apr 1993
N28 - Available from British Library Document Supply Centre- DSC:q94/23006

4. RCN - ngb9309508
EC - Department of the Environment, London (GB)
TI - Implementation of EC Directive 90/313 on the freedom of access to information
on the environment$bDraft regulations and guidance
PU - $cOct 1992
N28 - Available from British Library Document Supply Centre- DSC:MFE
N28 - Available from British Library Document Supply Centre- DSC:MFE

Summary: Grey literature

Advantages

Information not available in any other form

In some cases the material is free or reasonably cheap

Disadvantages

Notoriously difficult to get hold of as there is no standard way of classifying
it

Reference sources

There is not a large selection of dictionaries and encyclopaedias devoted to
environmental issues. This is unfortunate as they are an invaluable starting point
when investigating a new and unfamiliar topic. As mentioned earlier, the most
convenient method of identifying these publications is through the 'Books in Print'
directories.

In contrast to this there are a great number of useful directories specifically focused
on particular environmental areas. Directories are invaluable for details of
environmental organisations and companies. There are too many of these to

produce an exhaustive reference set here but a number of the key directories are included. They have been split into three main areas dealing with information sources, organisations and statistics.

Summary: directories, dictionaries and encyclopaedias

Advantages

Invaluable for quick reference enquiries

There are hundreds of good directories available

Easy access to details of environmental organisations and companies

Starting point to research when investigating new area

Disadvantages

They can be very expensive

Directories lose accuracy very quickly

Examples of useful reference sources:

Dictionaries/encyclopaedias

Dictionary of Ecology and Environment
P H Collin
P Collin Pub. London 1995
ISBN 0948549742

Earthwords: Dictionary of the Environment
Seymour Simon
Harper Collins Publishers. USA. 1995
ISBN 0060202343

Dictionary of Environmental Science and Technology
John Wiley and Sons Ltd, Chichester. 2nd ed. 1996
ISBN 0471960756

Dictionary of Environment and Sustainable Development
Alan Gilpin
John Wiley and Sons Ltd, Chichester. 1996
ISBN 0471962201

The Dictionary of Global Climatic Change
Compiled by W John Maunder
UCL Press Ltd. London. 1992
ISBN 1857280237

The Environmental Dictionary and Regulatory Cross-Reference
Compiled by James J King
John Wiley and Sons Inc. USA. 3rd ed. 1995
ISBN 0471119954

Environmental Glossary
David Dooley and Neil Kirkpatrick
PIRA International, 1993
ISBN 1858020158

The Wiley Encyclopaedia of Energy and the Environment
2 volume set
Edited by Attilio Bisio and Sharon Boots
John Wiley and Sons Inc. USA. 1997
ISBN 047114827X

Directories – secondary sources
ECO Directory of Environmental Databases in the United Kingdom
Monica Barlow and John Button
ECO Env. Info. Trust. Bristol. 1995.
ISBN 187466016
(Out of print now, but still a very useful source)

Environment Facts: a guide to using public registers of environmental information
Department of the Environment (now Department of Environment, Transport and
the Regions, DETR)
DOE. 1996 (free publication)
DOE, Publications Despatch Centre, Blackhorse Road, London SE99 6TT. Ref
No: 94 EP 335

Gale Directory of Databases (Volumes 1 and 2)
Volume 1: Online Databases
Volume 2: CD-ROM, Diskette, Magnetic Tape, Handheld and Batch Access
Database Products
Editor Kathleen Lopez Nolan
Gale Research Inc. Detroit
Vol 1 & 2: ISSN 1066-8934

DIRECTORIES/Yearbooks – organisations and issues
World Directory of Environmental Organisations, 5th ed.
Edited by TC Trzyna and Roberta Childers
Earthscan Publications, London, 1996
ISBN 185383307X

Directory of Environment and Development Issues
Network of Irish Environment & Development Organisations,
c/o 10 Upper Camden Street, Dublin 2, Republic of Ireland. 1995
ISBN 0952552108

ENDS Directory of environmental consultants
Annual Publication
ENDS Publications
ISBN 0907673120

Environmental Contacts: a guide for business
Department of Trade and Industry.
DTI. 1998 (free publication)

Environmental Health and Safety Yearbook
Institute of Environmental Health Officers
Environmental Health Publishers
ISBN 1872645045

The Environment Industry Yearbook 1998
Annual publication
Macmillan. London
ISBN 0333658116

Green Globe Yearbook 1997
Oxford University Press
ISBN 0198233485

Who's Who in the Environment: England; Northern Ireland; Scotland and Wales
Edited and updated by Kate Aldous and Rachel Adatia with Kim Milton
The Environment Council. London.
ISBN 0903158523 – England, 3rd ed. 1995
ISBN 0903158418 – Northern Ireland, 1994
ISBN 1853970190 – Scotland, 2nd ed. 1993
ISBN 0903158477 – Wales, 1995

World Who is Who and Does What in Environment & Conservation
Edited by Nicholas Polunin, complied by Lynn M Curme
Earthscan Publications, London, 1997
ISBN 1853833770

DIRECTORIES – statistics

Digest of Environmental Statistics, No. 19, 1997
Annual publication
Department of the Environment, Transport and the Regions
The Stationery Office (formerly HMSO). London.
ISBN 0117533998

The Environment in Your Pocket 1997
Annual publication
Department of the Environment, Transport and the Regions
The Stationery Office (formerly HMSO). London. (Free publication)
Available from: DoE, Publications Despatch Centre, Blackhorse Road,
London SE99 6TT Product Code: 97EP0023 EP

The European Environmental Statistics Handbook
Oksana Newman and Allen Foster
Gale Research International Ltd. London. 1993
ISBN 1873477665

Statistical Record of the Environment
Compiled and edited by Arsen J Darnay
Gale Research Inc. London and Detroit. 2nd ed. 1994
ISBN 0810388634

World Resources 1996-97 Database Disk
World Resource Institute
Earthscan Publications. London. 1996
ISBN 1853831004

Secondary sources

Secondary sources do not provide any original information of their own, instead they provide bibliographic details, and often an abstract, of the primary literature. The abstracting and indexing services of interest in the environmental area fall into three categories: those covering an area wider than the environment, those on the environment in general and those on specific aspects of the environment. Among the secondary sources, which include environmental topics in a wider field, are the following:

Chemical Abstracts
One of the largest, and oldest, of all abstracting services. It deals with all aspects of chemistry and chemical technology and is a comprehensive source of information on any aspect of the environment that has any connection with chemistry (which in practice covers a large number of environmental topics, e.g. pollution, hazardous chemicals, waste and recycling). It is less informative on other environmental topics such as conservation and environmental impact assessment. It covers books, periodicals, conference proceedings and patents in all major languages. Both manual and online versions are available, although the sheer bulk and cost of the printed version mean that few libraries are now able to subscribe to it. The indexes for 1987-1991 are available on CD-ROM. Chemicals/compounds can be searched using their unique Chemical Abstracts Registry Numbers, this simplifies the problem of compounds having multiple names.

Biological Abstracts
Good for biological aspects of the environment such as biodiversity and also for the effect of pollutants on the environment. Another very large database although not as big as *Chemical Abstracts*. The printed version is not particularly easy to use, so it is preferable to use the online or CD-ROM version (BIOSIS).

CAB Abstracts

The printed version consists of over 50 separate abstracting journals. Available online and on CD-ROM. Covers a wide range of environmental topics, not just agriculture. Examples are biodiversity, conservation, pesticides, renewable energy sources, environmental legislation, environmental policy, waste disposal, water quality, tourism and climatology. It has a very good coverage of developing world literature and includes topics such as rural economics.

Engineering Index

Available online and on CD-ROM as Compendex. Covers technology in general including many environmental topics such as transportation, building materials, flood control, water treatment, sanitary engineering, pollution and waste.

Georef, Geobase, Geoarchive

These three earth science indexing publications contain much useful material on environmental geology and geography. All three are available online and on CD-ROM.

ICONDA

A publication devoted to construction and civil engineering, which covers the environmental impact of construction projects. Available online and on CD-ROM.

Indexing journals devoted to the environment in general include two major titles:

Environment Abstracts

Available online and on CD-ROM as *Enviroline*. This covers all aspects of the environment including legislation and policy. This is the most comprehensive abstracting publication devoted solely to the environment.

Environmental Bibliography

Also available online and on CD-ROM. Also covers all aspects of the environment and should be used in conjunction with *Environment Abstracts*. Overlap between publications, even in the same subject area, can sometimes be surprisingly low so whenever possible it is advisable to use more than one source in order to obtain as much relevant information as possible. One disadvantage with *Environmental Bibliography* is that in the past it did not include abstracts. However, it is now beginning to add abstracts.

Finally, a selection of abstracting journals devoted to particular aspects of the environment include:

Pollution Abstracts

As the name suggests, this publication deals with all aspects of pollution. It is also available online and on CD-ROM.

Ecology Abstracts

This abstracting journal is devoted to the worldwide literature on ecology and the environment. Also available online and on CD-ROM.

In summary: abstracting and indexing publications

Advantages

        Provide subject, author and institution access point

        Save a huge amount of time

        One abstract may lead to new area of interest

        Often full abstract is included

        Covers much larger area than individual could

Disadvantages

        Reliance on the individual journals indexing policy and thesauri

        Possibly the most relevant journal is not covered

        Not all abstracting journals have a 'how to use' section

Chapter 4.   Electronic Sources

We are currently experiencing a revolution in the way information is published and distributed. Nowadays, we find more and more information arriving in some sort of electronic format rather than the traditional printed form. There are now examples of journals being exclusively produced in electronic format and new journals being made available exclusively through the Internet via a subscription service.

Electronic information retrieval is usually undertaken through online, CD-ROM or Internet media. Electronic databases can be searched in a greater variety of ways than manual sources and are more efficient to search. Concepts can be combined in a way that is impossible with printed sources and the search is interactive, allowing the searcher to refine the search. They also offer a potentially vast source of information, are more up-to-date and avoid the need for extensive storage space. On the other hand they can be expensive and, for online searching at least, need specialised searching skills. CD-ROM databases can be cheaper to use than online databases and require less skill but are not as current. In addition, several CD-ROM databases cannot be searched concurrently as is the case with online databases.

CD-ROM databases are usually obtained on a subscription basis, being updated at regular intervals (e.g. one month). Most CD-ROM, and online, databases are bibliographic but some are numerical, giving physical property data, and a few give the full text of articles.

As mentioned in Chapter 3, there are a number of important specialised secondary sources for environmental searchers. Databases such as *Enviroline*, *Environmental Bibliography* and *Pollution Abstracts* are the most popular. Even the more general databases such as *Chemical Abstracts*, *Compendex* and *CAB Abstracts* offer a wealth of information on environmental issues and should not be overlooked.

There are a number of primary source electronic databases that are known as databanks. Examples of such sources are: *ECDIN* (Environmental Chemicals Data Information Network); *Toxline*; *RTECS* (Registry of Toxic Effects of Chemical Substances) and *HSDB* (Hazardous Substances Data Bank) which supply the enquirer with data such as that concerning human and animal health, LD50 toxicity levels or the environmental fate of chemicals once they have been released into the environment. These databases supply a compendium of data that would be difficult and more time consuming to compile from other sources.

CD-ROM sources

The best reference source for CD-ROM titles is:

Gale Directory of Databases
Vol. 2: CD-ROM, Diskette, Magnetic Tape, Handheld and Batch Access Database
Products
Gale Research, Detroit, ISSN 1066-8934

A small selection of the CD-ROM titles applicable to the environment are as
follows:

Environment Abstracts (Enviroline)
Vendor: Bowker Electronic Publishing
Provides over 250,000 citations and abstracts of the world's periodical and other
published and unpublished literature dealing with environmental and energy-related
topics. Consists of three databases: *Acid Rain Abstracts*; *Energy Information Abstracts* and
Environment Abstracts.

Pollution Abstracts
Vendor: Cambridge Scientific Abstracts (CSA)
Contains more than 190,000 citations, with abstracts, to the worldwide technical
and non-technical literature on pollution research, sources and controls. Covers air,
water, land, thermal, noise, and radiological pollution; pesticides; sewage and waste
treatment; environmental action; toxicology and health.

Ecology Abstracts
Vendor: Cambridge Scientific Abstracts
Contains 175,000 citations, with abstracts, to the worldwide literature on ecology
and the environment. Focus is on how microbes, plants and animals interact with
each other and with the environment. Sources include specialist literature such as
journals, books, conference proceedings and reports.

Environmental Chemistry, Health & Safety
Vendor: The Royal Society of Chemistry
Contains citations, with abstracts, to published materials dealing with chemicals
deemed to cause actual or potential problems to humans or the environment,
including microbiological and radiation hazards. Records include chemical
substances and companies involved. Sources include journal articles, books,
technical reports, and other publications. Derived from the Royal Society of
Chemistry databases.

Water Resources Abstracts
Vendor: Silver Platter Information, Inc
Contains more than 250,000 citations, with abstracts, to scientific and technical
literature on the water resource-related aspects of the physical, social, and life
sciences. Covers related engineering and legal aspects of the characteristics,
conservation, control, use and management of water resources. Also covers the

nature of water and water cycles; water supply augmentation and conservation; water quality and quantity management and control; water resource planning, and engineering works.

Biosis Previews
Vendor: Biosis
Contains more than 10 million citations, with abstracts (for approximately 50% of the records) to worldwide literature on research in the life sciences: microbiology; plant and animal science; experimental medicine; agriculture; pharmacology; ecology; biochemistry and neurology. Covers original research reports, reviews of original research, history and philosophy or biology and biomedicine, and documentation and retrieval of biological information. Sources include approximately 6000 periodicals, as well as books, monographs, conference proceedings, research communications, symposia, reviews, notes and letters.

GEOBASE
Vendor: Elsevier Science
Contains more than 500,000 citations, with abstracts, to the worldwide literature on the earth sciences. Covers cartography, climatography, demography, ecology, environment, geography, geomorphology, natural resources, planning, regional studies, Developing world studies and transportation. Sources include journals, books, monographs, conference proceedings, reports, theses and dissertations.

CAB Health
Vendor: CAB International (CABI)
Contains 500,000 citations, with abstracts, to the world's research literature relating to human nutrition, parasitology, tropical medicine, environmental health. Covers English and foreign language journals, books, research reports, patents and standards and public health issues, and developing country literature.

AGRIS
Vendor: SilverPlatter Information Inc.
Contains more than 2.4 million citations (with abstracts for approx. 25% of the most recent citations) to the worldwide literature on all aspects of agriculture. Topics include: geography and history; legislation; education; economics, development, marketing and rural sociology, human nutrition, home economics and pollution.

Online sources
All of the aforementioned CD-ROM sources are available via online host providers such as *Dialog, Datastar, STN International.* A simple method of checking online availability of databases is to consult:

Gales Directory of Databases
Vol 1: Online Databases
Gale Research, Detroit
ISSN 1066-8934

Relative merits of CD-ROM vs online sources

There are three main options for electronic information retrieval: online, CD-ROM and online access through an Internet connection. All three have distinct advantages and disadvantages that need to be considered.

Traditional online information access

Access to the database hosts is on a subscription basis. The yearly subscription rates are generally low (e.g. *Dialog* – $72/year). The subscription gives the user a set of user manuals and information sheets for the databases accessible through the host. The use of the databases is on a pay-as-you-go basis and the costs vary from host to host and from database to database. The user normally pays for every minute of online time and each reference downloaded. In some databases there is a charge for each search term used, this is the case for *STN International* access to the database *Chemical Abstracts*.

Each database host has a slightly different searching language that the user must be familiar with when searching the databases. Even large hosts such as *Dialog* and *DataStar* have their own, very distinct, searching languages although they are owned by the same company *MAID*.

The great advantage of online searching is that the user may search many databases at the same time, thus saving time and money. There is a de-duplication command that allows the user automatically to exclude any duplicate references picked up and cheaper databases may be ranked in order of preference to ensure the duplicated reference is taken from the cheaper database.

The main disadvantage of online searching is that it cannot easily be performed by the end user. The enquirer must be well acquainted with the searching language of the host system. He/she must also be aware of the use of Boolean operators (And, Or or Not). This is essential as any mistakes incurred online can be very expensive. It is also helpful for the user to be reasonably familiar with the subject area s/he is searching in, as costly mistakes can be made when scientific or technological keywords are misunderstood or incorrectly used.

CD-ROM access

Individual CD-ROM titles are bought on either a one-off or a subscription basis. They usually offer Windows user-friendly software that can be used by end-users with the minimum of training.

The main disadvantage with CD-ROM searching is that the user may only search one database at a time. However, database searching incurs no extra cost however many references are downloaded, or mistakes made.

One other possible disadvantage with subscription-based CD-ROM titles is that occasionally the producer insists that the title is returned if the subscription is cancelled. This is in contrast to the situation where the subscription is cancelled to hard copy publications, where the subscriber is entitled to retain all back editions.

Multiple-user licences are available for most CD-ROM titles that will allow networking of the information over a number of terminals.

The advantage of CD-ROM technology is that there are no hidden costs once the title has been purchased. End users can search the databases without incurring any extra charges.

Internet online access

This method of access is very similar to online access except the databases are accessed through an Internet Web Browser. The subscription to the service is paid in the same way, the relevant home pages are accessed through a networked terminal and searching is performed through Windows driven software. At the time of going to print some datahosts are still charging for each minute the searcher is connected as well as for each reference downloaded, although this trend is diminishing. This can lead to high connect costs as the Internet can be very slow to respond to interrogation at certain times of the day.

Below is an example of a typical environmental search, carried out using the *Dialog Datahost* system and interrogating the databases: *Enviroline*; *Environmental Bibliography* and *Pollution Abstracts* simultaneously.

Example 5 – a typical online environmental topic search

A researcher is interested in finding recent journal articles on the subject of the role of peroxyacetyl nitrate as an atmospheric pollutant and its possible toxicity. His brief is to search for papers in English language only and within the time span 1990 onwards.

The first step of the search would be to interrogate the *Chemical Abstracts Registry* file to identify all possible chemical names and synonyms for the compound. After this has been achieved, all the names are added to the search strategy along with other relevant keywords such as atmosphere, atmospheric, pollutant, toxic, etc. The truncation, or wildcard, is used on any word that has the possibility of various endings. In the case of the Dialog system this is a question mark (?).

The various facets of the search are added together and the various restraints such as time scale and language are applied. Finally, as the enquirer is searching three databases at once, the duplicate removal command (RD) is used to ensure all retrieved references are unique. The search strategy and sample references are shown below.

```
Set  Items    Description
S1   3692     (PEROXYACETYL(W)NITRATE) OR PAN OR        (W) The keywords
               (ACETYL(W)PEROXYNITRATE)                   must appear next
               OR (METHYLCARBONYL(W)PEROXYNITRATE)            to each other
S2   39113    (AIR OR ATMOSPHERE?)(S)POLLUTANT?      (S) The keywords must
S3   28       S1 AND S2                                be in the same sentence
S4   1726795  TOXIC? OR HAZARD? OR EFFECT?
S5   125      S3 AND S4
S6   45       S5/1990:1997
S7   38       S6 AND LA=ENGLISH                     LA = Language descriptor
S8   27       RD (unique items)
```

Example output:

10/9/7   (Item 7 from file: 40)
DIALOG(R)File 40:Enviroline(R)
(c) 1997 Congressional Information Service. All rts. reserv.

00394614 ENVIROLINE NUMBER: 92-05147
Observations of H2O2 and PAN in a Rural Atmosphere
Dollard, G. J.; Davies, T. J., AEA Environ & Energy, Oxford, UK
Environ Pollut v75, n1, p45(8)
1992
JOURNAL ANNOUNCEMENT: 19920500
DOCUMENT TYPE: research article LANGUAGE: English
ABSTRACT: Hydrogen peroxide and PAN are formed by photochemical reactions
in the atmosphere. A four-yr study of the concentrations of these compounds
over a rural section of southern England demonstrated seasonal and diurnal
patterns for both. Concentrations were affected by wind direction and
temperature. Hydrogen peroxide concentration is increasing with time and
with ozone formation as would be expected, since it is produced during
ozonization. With a global model that uses both latitude and altitude, two
future growth scenarios were predicted. Both demonstrate increases in H2O2,
but the amount is somewhat less for a low-growth scenario. During
photochemical episodes, the formation sequence is O3, PAN, H2O2. Thus,
vegetation can be exposed to peak concentrations of these pollutants in
rapid succession with possible adverse effects on plant tissues.
SPECIAL FEATURES: 3 diagram(s); 6 graph(s); 28 reference(s)
MAJOR DESCRIPTORS: HYDROGEN PEROXIDE; PEROXYACETYL NITRATE;
  RURAL ATMOSPHERE; OZONE; AIR POLLUTION EFFECTS; OXIDANTS;

MONITORING, AIR; DIURNAL CHANGES; SEASONAL COMPARISONS;
PHOTOCHEMISTRY
MINOR DESCRIPTORS: DAYTIME-NIGHTTIME COMPARISONS; SMOG,
PHOTOCHEMICAL;
HYDROCARBONS, AIR; POLLUTION FORECASTING
REVIEW CLASSIFICATION: 01

10/9/11   (Item 1 from file: 41)
DIALOG(R)File 41:Pollution Abs

231706 96-09703
    Effects of air pollutants (PAN, nitrogen oxides, sulfur dioxide, ozone,
chlorine and fluoride) on the plants
    Halek, F.
    Materials and Energy Res. Cent., P.O. Box 14155-4777, Tehran, Iran
    1995 European Aerosol Conference Helsinki (Finland) 18-22 Sep 1995
    J. AEROSOL SCI VOL. 26, p. S397, Publ.Yr: 1995
    SUMMARY LANGUAGE – ENGLISH
    Languages: ENGLISH
    Journal Announcement: V27N10
    Gaseous Pollutants resulting from combustion of fuels and other human
activities which are daily increasing in urban air, are affecting plant
metabolisms and causing plants diseases. In this study pollutants such as
Ozone, Peroxyacetyl Nitrate (PAN), Nitrogen Oxides, Sulfur dioxide,
Chlorine and fluoride have been investigated on several plants. This study
also indicates that depending on the nature of the pollutants, and their
concentrations and time of exposure, causes different damages to plants
from reduction of growth rate to death of the plant.
    Descriptors: air pollution; pollution effects; nitrogen oxides; sulfur
dioxide; ozone; chlorine; fluoride; peroxyacetyl nitrate; plants; growth;
mortality

Chapter 5.   Internet Sources

The Internet's history and growth is well documented elsewhere and so will not be discussed here. This chapter will concentrate on Internet sources for environmental information searching.

The range of environmental information on the Internet is huge; much larger than within any other scientific discipline except perhaps medicine. The Internet and its resources have been separated from the chapter on other electronic media as there is a distinct difference in the type of information available from Internet or World Wide Web sources.

As mentioned earlier, the majority of electronic sources act as secondary sources of information, simply reporting on details of primary source information. The Internet is different in that the material now available almost matches the range of material available in other formats. For example, there are electronic journals; searchable databases and library catalogues; email discussion groups and bulletin boards; up-to-date environmental texts and documents; technical reports and conference proceedings; computer software, images and sound archives that can be downloaded. This allows the environmental enquirer a larger range of sources than any other single medium.

In addition, most of the active environmental organisations and government agencies now have their own home pages on the Internet. Institutions from Greenpeace to the US EPA have information about themselves and other related organisations easily accessible through their home page. Some pages even have searchable data banks available and hence one is able to explore individual topics. Sometimes even images can be accessed and downloaded without copyright restrictions.

One of the most useful functions of the Internet, however, is its ability to put people in touch with experts and other interested parties in most environmental fields around the world. Through the use of email it is possible to join pertinent discussion groups and bulletin boards that focus on your topic of interest. Within the groups one will find experts from academia, commerce and industry who specialise in the area. A word of caution here, one must be very selective in choosing discussion groups, some of them are very active and produce copious amounts of correspondence that may not be of any relevance.

How to assess usefulness of information

Locating environmental information can be difficult and time-consuming and in some instances the information proves worthless. There is a need to assess quality and efficacy of information found on the Internet and, with this aim in mind, the British Library has drawn up criteria to help the user assess the usefulness of sources.

Criteria

1. Purpose   Factual, informative, subjective, affiliations
2. Authority   A well regarded institution or a student's home page?
3. Scope   Specialised, in-depth, wide-ranging, superficial
4. Currency   Check for last update to pages if currency is vital
5. Uniqueness   How many other pages have the same information?
6. Accessibility Easy to access and quick to download?
7. Accuracy   If possible, check accuracy with other sources
8. Audience   Do the pages state their intended audience?
9. Format   Do pages have the option of text only as well as graphics option

Some useful UK and European internet sites

There are fifteen UK and European sites of wide environmental interest listed below. They consist of a mixture of governmental, NGO and charity sites. A short description of each of the organisations is included. Each site has been evaluated using the criteria outlined earlier. Other sites are obtainable by linking through to the British Library's Environmental Information Service Home Page at:
http://www.bl.uk/services/sris/eis/

Department of the Environment, Transport and the Regions Home Page
http://www.detr.gov.uk/
Official DETR pages, becoming increasingly useful as more detailed information is added. Includes, for example, pages of information on air pollution levels across the UK (updated hourly), a forecast of air quality within UK cities and an explanation of the chemistry of the main atmospheric pollutants.

Environmental Change Network (ECN)
http://mwnta.nmw.ac.uk/ecn/index.html
ECN is the UK's integrated long-term environmental monitoring network. It is designed to collect, store, analyse and interpret long-term data based on a set of key physical, chemical and biological variables which drive and respond to environmental change.

Natural Environment Research Council
http://www.nerc.ac.uk/
The mission of the Natural Environment Research Council is: to promote and support, by any means, high quality basic, strategic and applied research, survey, long-term environmental monitoring and related postgraduate training in terrestrial, marine and freshwater biology and Earth, atmospheric, hydrological, oceanographic and polar sciences and Earth observations.

Global Environmental Network for Information Exchange in the UK (GENIE)
http://www-genie.mrrl.lut.ac.uk/
The GENIE project provides a system for locating and accessing relevant information on Global Environmental Change. The facility will be a vital part of

the UK contribution to international science programmes including projects within the International Geosphere-Biosphere Programme (IGBP), the World Climate Research Programme (WCRP) and the Human Dimensions of Global Environmental Change Programme (HDGECP).

Institute of Terrestrial Ecology
http://www.nmw.ac.uk:80/ite/
One of four institutes which form the Centre of Ecology and Hydrology, a part of the UK Natural Environment Research Council responsible for research into all aspects of the terrestrial environment. Disseminates data sets regarding various aspects of the UK countryside

UK Environment Agency Homepage
http://www.environment-agency.gov.uk/
The Environment Agency World Wide Web Home Page is currently being developed. A key feature of this site is the State of the Environment report: this is a snapshot look at the pressures on the environment and how the quality of the environment has changed over the last twenty-five or so years. This web site will be regularly updated and enhanced to provide comprehensive information and advice on the protection and management of the environment. Look in the information and resource pages for details on how to contact them.

ENDS Homepage
http://www.ends.co.uk/
ENDS provides accurate and independent intelligence on the environment for anybody with a professional interest in environmental affairs, whether in the business, academic, regulatory or campaigning communities. They focus primarily on the UK and Europe.

PRISM/WRF Homepage
http://www.wrfound.org.uk/index.html
PRISM is the information service of the World Resource Foundation (WRF), dedicated to providing a worldwide database on integrated, sustainable waste management. One of the Foundation's objective is to stimulate an effective debate into this important area of society's use of resources.

The UK Environment in Facts and Figures
http://www.detr.gov.uk/doe/envir/epsim/index.htm
Information on the state of the environment is published by DETR (formerly DOE) in a number of statistical reports: the *Digest of Environmental Statistics* and *The UK Environment* being the principal ones. Some of the key facts and figures which underpin these publications are presented on these pages in order to widen the availability of environmental information and also to make it easier for users, both in the UK and abroad, to access and manipulate data for analysis.

Booknet – New environmental titles
http://www.nhbs.co.uk:80/booknet/nb132.html
Home of the world's biggest environmental bookstore, supplying private
individuals, scientists, other academics, libraries, NGOs, IGOs, environment
professionals and government agencies. Search, browse and order from NHBS
BOOKNET, a descriptive catalogue of over 40,000 in-print or forthcoming
environment-related books, CD-ROMs and other materials. BookNet offers
powerful search facilities as well as browsing by subject and geographical area.
Orders can be placed by email. These pages of the Natural History Book Store
(NHBS) are devoted to new book titles in the environmental area.

UNED-UK Home page
http://www.oneworld.org/uned-uk/
The United Nations Environment and Development UK Committee is the
successor to the United Nations Environment Programme UK (UNEP-UK), first
established as UNEP's National Committee in 1987.

World Conservation Monitoring Centre
http://www.wcmc.org.uk/emergency/
During 'environmental emergencies', such as major fires or oil spills, WCMC is able
to provide relevant environmental information rapidly to support the activities of
those responsible for coping with the problems that arise. These pages show
examples of incidents in which the WCMC were able to provide assistance.
Current incidents are also reported on their Late News pages.

European Environment Agency
http://www.eea.dk/
The goal of the EEA and its wider network, EIONET, is to provide the European
Union and the Member States with high quality information for policy-making
and assessment of the environment, to inform the general public, and to provide
scientific and technical support to these ends.

The Environment Council Homepage
http://www.greenchannel.com/tec
The Environment Council is a non governmental organisation and registered
charity based in London which exists to enhance and protect the quality and
diversity of Britain's environment for present and future generations through
building awareness, dialogue, understanding and effective action.

The Environment Agency Public Registers Page
http://www.environment-agency.gov.uk/info/registers.html#registers
Under the legislation for many of its functions, the Agency must maintain a set of
Public Registers. Information is held in a combination of paper and computer files
which may be inspected at the Agency's Regional and Area offices.

Chapter 7.   The British Library's Environmental Information Service

The British Library holds a large selection of environmental titles and journals. It must be pointed out that the British Library London Reading Rooms are not lending libraries, but it is possible to photocopy most articles or passages (subject to copyright laws). To obtain loans of books and journals, the enquirer must use the interlibrary loan facility available through the British Library's Document Supply Centre (Boston Spa site).

The Environmental Information Service (EIS) was established in 1989. It acts as a gateway to the British Library's environmental holdings and hopes to answer the majority of the environmental enquirer's needs.

The section offers a number of services within the environmental field. Its remit includes all sectors of the community from the general public and students through to industry, consultancies, international agencies and government offices.

Environmental Enquiry point
This service is designed to supply immediate answers to enquiries about names and addresses of environmental organisations, suppliers and specialists. In addition, checks on literature held by the library on environmental issues can be undertaken and results posted. Bibliographies of specified subject areas can be prepared using the British Library catalogues. One of the aims of EIS is to be a signposting service, where people come with specific enquiries and EIS then attempts to put them in touch with the most relevant person or organisation.

The enquiry point is free at the point of use. However, if an enquiry turns out to be involved and/or will take up a large percentage of staff time, then the enquirer will be informed that a charge will have to be made to help recover basic staffing and other costs.

Online priced enquiry service
Through STMsearch EIS provides expert literature searches covering all areas of the environment as well as other areas such as science, technology and medicine. With skilled online searchers and access to over 400 databases, the service provides quick and cost-effective access to information. The initial consultation is free and a quotation is then given for the search itself.

All of the major environmental databases are accessible through STMsearch. For example, *Enviroline, Environmental Bibliography, Aqualine, Pollution Abstracts, ECDIN, Oceanic Abstracts, Toxline, CAB Abstracts*.

Environmental information courses
The environmental course Sources of Environmental Information is run approximately three times each year and offers participants a day long lecture

course on the different aspects of environmental information. Included in the day is a series of lectures from British Library staff on various sources of information; an Internet lecture and demonstration of environmental sources available; a series of case study lectures from external speakers from various environmental areas and a number of demonstrations of databases and online systems. In addition, participants are given a demonstration of the EIS internet home pages.

There is also a one-day Environmental Information on the Internet seminar for people who require more in-depth information and hands-on experience of Internet resources. For more information, contact: Dave Dubuisson, Marketing Department, Tel No: 0171 412 7470.

Environmental publications
The British Library also produces a number of publications on environmental issues. Recent titles on the environment include: *Environmental information – a guide to sources* (2nd ed.), *Environmental auditing* and *Freight transport and the environment*. For more details and an order form, contact: Paul Wilson, Marketing Department, Tel No: 0171 412 7472.

Environmental Information Service home page
The EIS home page is the most recent addition to the range of services offered. Over the last year, EIS has been making extensive use of the Internet for answering free enquiries, presently 40% of free enquiries are answered this way. As a natural progression from its use of the Internet, it was thought appropriate that EIS should develop its own home page to help Internet users locate relevant environmental information for themselves.

The EIS home page consists of the following items:

Information on other sources
> EIS has used many other organisations' home pages and databases when researching environmental topics. Here lists are supplied of other organisations in alphabetical order. Most organisations are accompanied by a paragraph briefly listing what their pages contain and what their main interests are.

Hypertext links to useful organisations
> Through hypertext links an enquirer can be connected to any of the organisations included in the alphabetical listing.

Contact details:
> Environmental Information Service
> The British Library
> 25 Southampton Buildings
> London WC2A 1AW

> Tel No: 0171 412 7955
> Fax No: 0171 412 7954
> email: eis@bl.uk
> **http://www.bl.uk/services/sris/eis/**

Glossary of Terms

Boolean operator – A logical term used for combining concepts used in information searching. The three operators are AND, OR and NOT.

Command language – A specialist computing language for use in online searching. It always includes the three Boolean operators (see above), as well as commands for various operations.

Database – Any file of information formatted as a series of discrete 'entries' can be called a database, but the term is usually used for files stored electronically. Most abstracting and indexing services are now stored in this way, and may be searched 'online'.

Descriptor – A 'key word' added to an entry in a database, to identify its subject matter. Many databases have a list of permitted descriptors, called a thesaurus.

Field identifiers – These allow the database searcher to locate keywords only in selected fields, e.g. title field (/TI), geographical location (/GL) or author field (/AU)

Host – A commercial company that mounts databases on a mainframe computer, with a link to the international telephone network so that subscribers may search the databases using their own desktop computers.

Primary source – Any journal or book containing original information that has not previously been published elsewhere.

Secondary source – A publication that summarises information that has previously been published in a primary source. For example, an abstracting or indexing service.

Truncation – A symbol, usually a $, # or ?, used at the beginning, or end, of a search term that instructs the database to retrieve all beginnings or endings of the term. For example, the term '#pollut#' would retrieve pollute, polluting, pollution and anti-polluting.

Wildcard – Same as truncation, but can also be used in the middle of a word. For example, fertili?er will retrieve both American (fertilizer) and British (fertiliser) spellings of the word.